ADVENTURES IN COLONIAL AMERICA

THE VILLAGE

Life in Colonial Times

by James E. Knight

illustrated by Jan Palmer

Cover art by Shi Chen.

Library of Congress Cataloging-in-Publication Data

Knight, James E.
   The village.

   Summary: Describes the lives and occupations of an
early eighteenth-century New Jersey farming village.
   1. New Jersey—Social life and customs—Colonial
period, ca. 1600–1775—Juvenile literature.   2. City
and town life—New Jersey—Juvenile literature.
3. United States—Social life and customs—Colonial
period, ca. 1600–1775—Juvenile literature. [1. New
Jersey—Social life and customs—Colonial period, 1600–
1775.   2. United States—Social life and customs—
Colonial period, 1600–1775]   I. Palmer Jan, ill.
II. Title.
F137.K56   974.9'02   81-23084
ISBN 0-89375-728-4 (lib. bdg.)   AACR2
ISBN 0-8167-4800-4 (pbk.)

This edition published 1998 by Troll Communications L.L.C.

Printed in the United States of America.

10   9   8   7   6   5   4   3   2

THE VILLAGE

Life in Colonial Times

The little village of Glenn Creek began like many other colonial towns of New Jersey, or West Jersey, as it is often called. In 1715, a group of settlers arrived from Scotland. They set up their small homes and shops on the banks of the stream that wound through the fertile farmland. Some English and Irish colonists followed.

Now, in 1730, the village has become a center for the farmers in the area. They travel to Glenn Creek for their milling, coopering, and other needs.

About an hour's travel downstream, the creek itself empties into the Delaware River. There the rivermen load their boats with farm produce and grain. They float these goods down to Trenton Falls and then to the market in Philadelphia.

As in any colonial town, the people of Glenn Creek depend on one another. If they don't have something they need, they cannot send off to the "big city" or back to England or Scotland to get it. They make almost everything they use. They have to. And so, everybody works—men and women and some children, too. They work long, hard hours—some in the fields, some in the houses, some in the mill, some in the shops. They all work together, and that's why Glenn Creek is growing.

Probably the town's most important business is the gristmill. It was the first business to be established here. Sandy Selkirk picked out a spot on the creek and dammed it up to turn his water wheel. Then farmers from all around began to come to Sandy's gristmill to grind their grain. Soon, other shops opened up nearby. And before long, Glenn Creek became a village.

But it all began with Sandy's gristmill. The mill's water wheel harnesses the power of the creek and uses it to turn the huge stones of the gristmill. The mill has only one pair of grinding stones. That's all the water power Sandy can get from Glenn Creek. The granite millstones were dug out of a nearby hillside. They sit one on top of the other with a spindle, or axle, through them. The bottom stone, called the bedder, does not turn. The top stone, called the runner, turns and grinds against the bedder. When grain is placed between the two stones, it is ground into fine flour.

When Sandy first set up his mill, it was out-of-doors. But in the winter, when the creek froze, the water wheel would not turn. So Sandy built a shed right over the mill. That keeps the water from freezing.

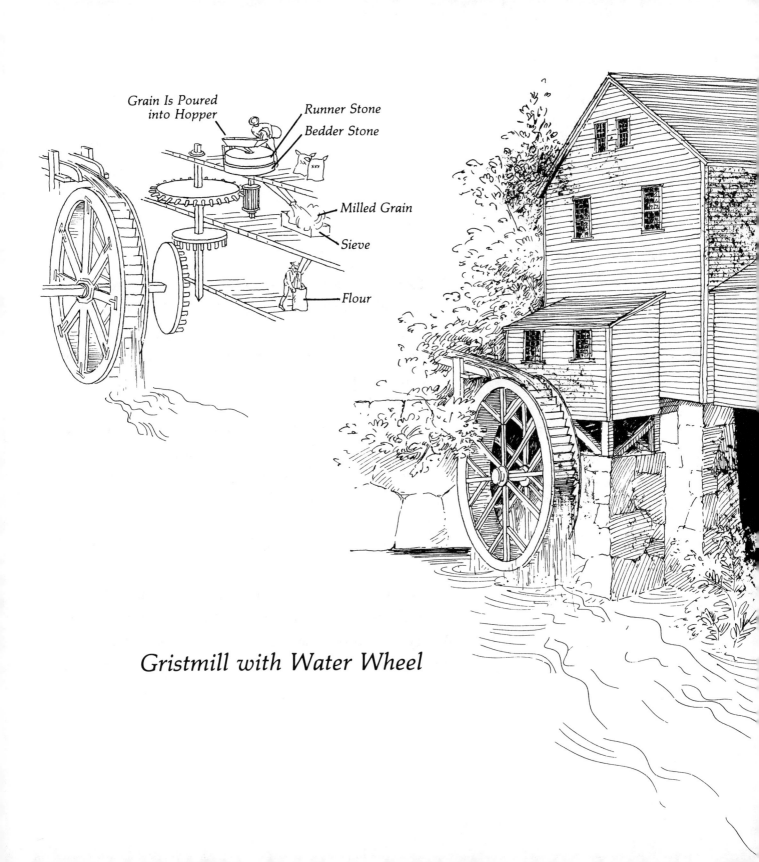

Grain Is Poured
into Hopper

Runner Stone

Bedder Stone

Milled Grain

Sieve

Flour

Gristmill with Water Wheel

Pancake Turner

Meat Fork

Door Latch

Saturday is a busy time at the gristmill. That's when the farmers usually arrive with their grain. Sandy takes the grain on a first-come, first-served basis. So if two farmers arrive together, there may be an argument over who goes first.

The grain sacks are unloaded from the farmer's wagon and pulled up to the top floor of the mill by a pulley. Then the grain is poured into a funnel-shaped box called a hopper. From the hopper it moves down through a hole onto the bedder stone. The runner stone turns, and the grain becomes flour.

Like all millers in the Colonies, Sandy takes his pay from what he grinds. He keeps one-eighth of the flour or one-sixth of the cornmeal that comes out of his mill.

Right next to the gristmill is the blacksmith's forge. Henry Kirkwood, the blacksmith, planned it that way. Henry knew that while the farmers were waiting for their grain to be made into flour, they could have their horses shod at his shop. Or they could have a plow repaired or a new axe made. And Henry was right.

The heart of Henry's blacksmith shop is the forge. It took him nearly a year to build it. The forge, the chimney, and the hood over the fire pit are made of local stone. At the back of the forge is a pipe for the bellows. The bellows is a collapsible bag made of leather and wood. Henry uses the bellows to blow air into the forge. This makes the charcoal in the fire pit white hot.

Henry can make almost anything a farmer needs. First, he heats up a piece of iron in his forge until it is red hot. Then he places it on his heavy iron anvil and hammers it into shape. Each time his hammer strikes the hot metal, sparks shoot through the air. He can make nearly anything the people of Glenn Creek need, too—knives, hide scrapers, hoes, rakes, and even cowbells!

But most of Henry's business is shoeing horses. He makes his own horseshoes from iron, and he makes his own nails, too. There are a lot of horses that need shoeing in the American Colonies.

Blacksmith at His Forge

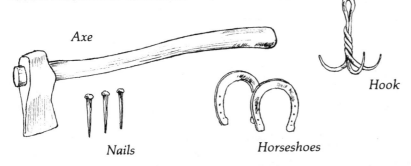

Axe

Nails

Horseshoes

Hook

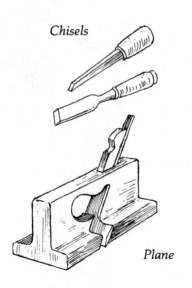

Chisels

Plane

Most of the other businesses of Glenn Creek are in the center of the village on High Street. Down at one end is George Crampian's workshop and storage shed. George is a housewright, or carpenter. A housewright makes and builds frames for houses. George certainly does that, but in a small town like Glenn Creek he does lots of other things, too. He is a "joiner"—he joins wood together into things like cupboards and staircases. He makes his own paint and his own furniture. But house framing is what he does best.

When George is ready to build a house, he picks the best oak trees he can find for lumber. Glenn Creek doesn't have a sawmill, and the nearest one is thirty miles away. So George and his apprentice must chop the trees into timbers. The axes they use were made on Henry Kirkwood's forge.

When the timbers have all been cut, George and his apprentice lay them out on the ground and join them.

Nails are very expensive. So George makes his own—actually his apprentice makes them. They are called

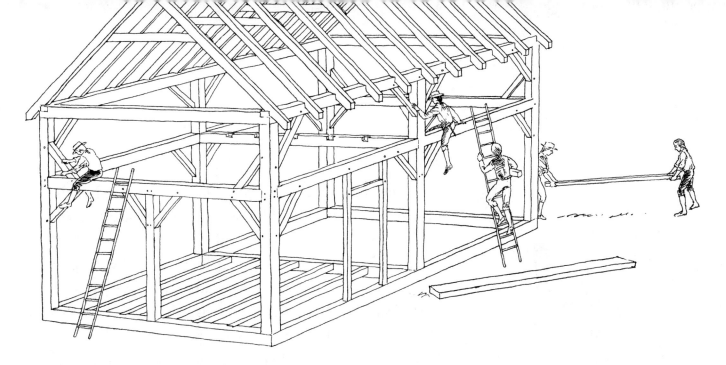

"trunnels," and they are made from hardwood, like hickory. When George joins the posts and beams of the house together, he nails them with trunnels.

Trunnels

Then George and his workers have a "house raising." The men use long poles, called pikes, to push up the whole frame. Soon the frame of the house is standing. Then George must stiffen it by adding braces. He fills in the spaces between the posts with rough bricks and mortar. The frame is usually covered with clapboards. Next come the peak frames and rafters. Then the apprentice cuts shingles for the roof. And, in just a few days' time, there stands a brand-new home.

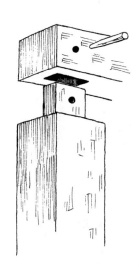

*Curved Froe for
Cutting Staves*

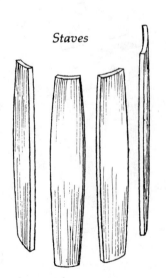

Staves

After the outside is complete, George usually does the inside work, too. He builds the walls for the rooms, and he adds the window sashes and stairs.

Like the miller, the carpenter doesn't usually get paid for a house in cash. There is very little cash money in such a small town. The housewright usually takes his fee in "country pay." It may be smoked hams or farm crops or tanned leather. Sometimes it takes the new homeowner years to finish paying the housewright.

Down from George Crampian's workshop, past the schoolhouse, is the cooper's shed. Angus Mull is usually in there, hard at work. He is one of the busiest of the workers in Glenn Creek, because he is the only cooper for forty miles around. Coopers make pails and kegs and tubs and barrels. And farmers need lots of them.

Angus makes two kinds of barrels. "Wet" barrels are for storing cider, syrup, molasses, and other liquids. Dry, or "slack," barrels are for storing grain, apples, flour, or cornmeal.

The staves of a barrel are the most important part. They are the upright pieces. Angus doesn't make his own

12

Sap Carrier

The Cooper

Small Barrel with
Wooden Hoops

Container for
Flour or Sugar

Pounding in the
Barrel Head with a Mallet

staves. Farmers make them during the winter by splitting oak logs. In return for the staves, the farmers pay a lower price for the barrels they buy from Angus.

Angus uses thin oak staves for dry barrels and thick staves for wet barrels. He must shape them properly before they can be used. A stave must be broad in the middle, tapered at the ends, and slightly curved. If the staves aren't curved, the barrel won't bulge in the middle the way it should.

Trimming Edges
with Chamfer Knife

After Angus has shaped the staves, he puts the barrel together. He stands several staves inside a wooden hoop. With a rope, he pulls the staves close and even. Then he drives another hoop over the top of them, so they are forced together tightly.

Now the rough edges must be trimmed off and the barrel head put on. Angus makes a barrel head out of two boards pegged together. He draws a circle on the boards and cuts it out with his saw. Then he taps in the head with his mallet, turns the barrel right side up, and it is ready to use.

Angus enjoys his work, but he thinks ahead, too. He believes that one day, barrels will be made with iron hoops instead of wooden ones. Iron, he says, will make the barrels much stronger.

Right across from the cooper's shed is where John Selkirk spends his time. John, who is Sandy's brother, is the village potter.

The Potter

John cannot make the stronger type of pottery—called "stoneware"—because that takes special clay and special heating. For stoneware goods, the townspeople must go to New York or Philadelphia. But most of them are happy with John's "redware" pottery. It is made from the fine-textured, red brick clay found in the nearby creek bed.

You can usually find John in one of two places—digging a new supply of clay or hunched over his potter's wheel. The potter's wheel is a small table attached by an

Pure Clay

One Part Sand Added to Four Parts Clay

axle to a wheel near the floor. When John kicks the wheel, the table spins.

First, John must make sure the clay is clean—free of twigs or dirt. This is pure clay, which would crack when heated. So he "tempers" it, or makes it stronger, by adding one part white sand to four parts clay. Then the mixture must dry for at least a week. Next, John beats it into a wet, soft mass to get rid of any air bubbles. Then it's ready for the potter's wheel.

The wheel spins around, and John begins to shape the clay into a bowl or a plate or a pitcher. He is an artist at work. When the piece is finished, it is put out to dry on a drying board.

When the bowl or pitcher is dry, it must be "fired" in an oven called a kiln. The pottery stays in the kiln for a day or so over a hot wood fire. Then the kiln must cool very slowly. Otherwise the pottery will crack.

When the pottery is cool, John "glazes" it, or covers it, with a mixture of sand, water, and red lead. When the glaze is dry, the pieces are put back into the kiln and fired again. Now the pottery is ready to be used.

Kneading Clay to Remove Air Bubbles

Kiln

17

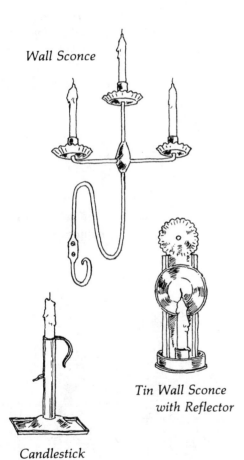

Wall Sconce

Tin Wall Sconce
with Reflector

Candlestick

A short walk past the potter's shed is Martha Hamilton's chandlery. Martha's workshop is really just a room in her house, but she is one of the best candlemakers in the whole colony. In fact, the traveling chandlers from Philadelphia have stopped coming to Glenn Creek. Nobody wants their candles if they can have Martha's.

Martha does not have the big candle molds that are used for candlemaking in Philadelphia. But she is very skilled at her craft. All year long, she saves fat from the meat of hogs, beef, or sheep. Then she melts it down in a heavy crock, until it is hot tallow. The candlewicks are made from linen.

Martha dips each wick into a container of hot tallow. Between dips, the tallow that is stuck to the wick is allowed to cool. Martha dips the wicks over and over again. When they are coated with enough tallow, and they are the right thickness, Martha hangs the candles up to cool.

Martha Hamilton is always busy. Everyone in the village needs candles. And besides her chandlery, Martha must run her house and tend to her children. Her hours are

Candlemaking

Linen Wicks

Hot Tallow

Drying Rack

long and hard. But all of the women in Glenn Creek work long, hard hours. There are very few comforts in colonial homes.

A Christening

Leather Goods

Work Apron

Shoes

Gaiters

Not far away from Martha Hamilton's is St. Andrew's Church, in the center of Glenn Creek. Reverend Isaac Tate is one of the village founders. He sailed from Scotland with the Selkirks and others. The Reverend holds Sunday services and Wednesday-night Bible classes. And, of course, he sees to weddings and christenings and funerals, too.

There is one other very important business in the village of Glenn Creek. It is Saul Swithin's tannery, about half a mile downstream from the mill. The reason it is so far away from the town is because the odor of Saul's tanning vats and drying racks can be overpowering. Even so, if the wind is blowing in the right direction, the whole town can smell the tanner at work!

Nearly everyone in a colonial town needs leather. Farmers need boots. Craftspeople need work aprons. Men, women, and children need shoes, belts, saddles, and harnesses. They keep Saul hard at work.

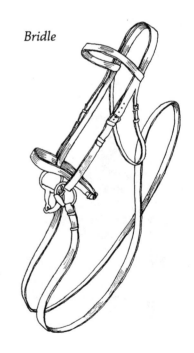

Bridle

There are two kinds of tanners: skin tanners and hide tanners. A skin tanner works with skins of pigs or sheep or deer. There is a skin tanner in the next county. Saul is a hide tanner. He works with the hides of oxen, horses, and cows.

When a customer brings a hide to the tannery, Saul splits it down the middle and scratches the customer's initials on it. Then he soaks it in water to soften it. Next he throws it on a stack of other hides. After a few days, he scrapes the hide to get rid of the hair.

A tannery uses lots of water. That explains why Saul built his tannery right on the creek. He has six large vats, which he must fill with water. The hides are put in the vats, and tannic acid is added. This toughens the hides. Saul gets the tannic acid from a tanbark mill about twenty miles away. It is made from bark stripped off black-oak or hemlock trees. The bark is ground into grains.

The longer the hides stay in the solution of tannic acid and water, the tougher they become. For shoe leather, Saul may keep the hides in the vats for as long as a year.

The Tanner

*Removing Hair from
a Hide with Unhairing Knife*

*Using a Currier's Knife to
Scrape and Soften Hide
after Tanning*

How does Saul know when the hides are ready to come out of the vats? He can tell by "touch." The hides must be just soft enough and just pliable enough. When Saul judges that the leather is ready to be used, he takes it out of the vat. Then he washes it in the creek and hangs it up to dry on the racks. He beats each hide from time to time with a heavy stick to make it more pliable.

When the leather is ready, Saul returns half of it to the customer who brought him the hide. For payment, he keeps the other half. He may sell it to someone else, or he may use it to make a pair of boots or shoes. You see, Saul is also the village shoemaker.

Back in town is Dan Gordon's print shop. All the people who live in and around Glenn Creek depend on Dan for newsletters and for each year's copy of *The Jersey Almanack*. The *Almanack* is filled with all sorts of information. It forecasts the weather. It lists the arrivals and departures of ships, ferries, and coaches. And it tells the farmers the best times for planting and harvesting crops. Besides all that, everyone enjoys reading the *Almanack*'s collection of jokes, riddles, and proverbs.

A lot of work goes into every piece of paper that Dan Gordon prints. First, Dan and his apprentice must set the type. When Dan came to America, he brought his most valuable possession with him—a large, heavy case filled with hundreds of small metal letters. These letters are the type Dan uses to print from.

Letter by letter, Dan must set type for each word in his newsletters and *Almanack*. He places the letters in a line in a small wooden tray. When all the lines of type are ready, they are hammered into place in a large wooden frame, so they will not move.

Next, Dan and his apprentice prepare the printing press. The frame of this big, heavy machine is made of oak. Its moving parts are made of metal. When the trays of type are ready, they are placed on the "bed" of the press. Dan's apprentice puts ink on the type, and Dan pulls a lever that presses the paper against the type. Then the printed sheet of paper is lifted off the press and inspected.

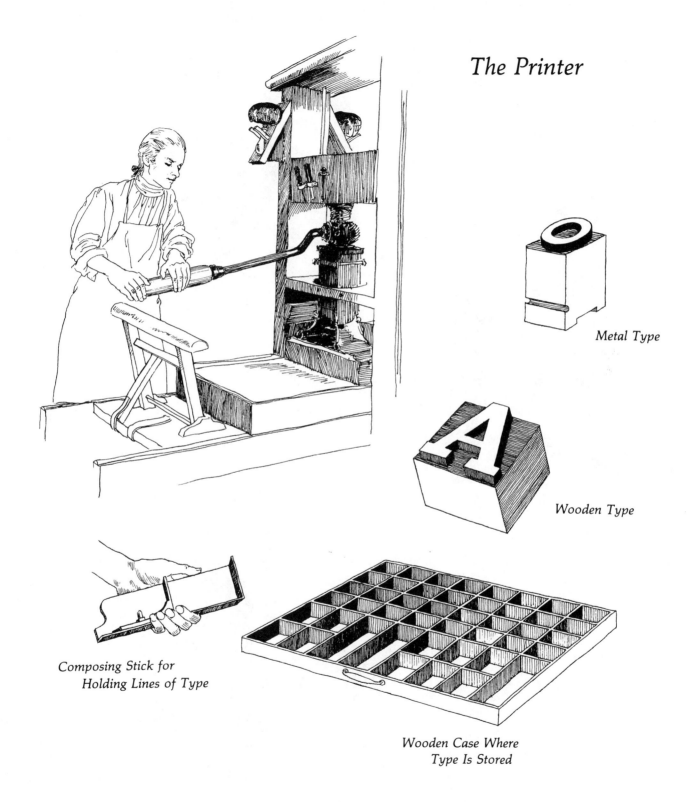

The Printer

Metal Type

Wooden Type

Composing Stick for
Holding Lines of Type

Wooden Case Where
Type Is Stored

So Dan's work is really several jobs. He is a writer, typesetter, proofreader, and printer. But it is not unusual that Dan does more than one job. Lots of villagers "do something else on the side." This is the only way to get things done in Colonial America.

When Sandy Selkirk is not milling, he and his wife run a small bakery at the side of the gristmill. In his spare time, John Selkirk glazes windows for George Crampian's houses. If George is not working on a house, he is busy building stone walls or steps. When the school teacher is sick or away, Martha Hamilton fills in. Saul Swithin is both tanner and shoemaker. Henry Kirkwood, the blacksmith, is also the veterinarian and the dentist! And Angus Mull, the cooper, built a small ferryboat in his spare time last year. So when he is not busy making barrels, he ferries people back and forth across the Delaware River.

There is hardly a person in town who does *not* hold down two jobs. That explains why most of the townspeople stop off at Reverend Tate's house from time to time. They are not there for services. It seems that when he came over from Scotland, the Reverend brought a fine set of steel scissors with him. So in his spare time, Reverend Isaac Tate is Glenn Creek's favorite barber.

Index

*(Page numbers that appear in **boldface** type refer to illustrations.)*